It's All in the Mind:
Think Differently, Get Fit, Change Your Life

Jacqueline Kelly

DEDICATION

So many people deserve a shout-out on this very important page in my first book. I hope you all know who you are. When I read these pages over and over, who I really want to dedicate it to is my mom. You are a part of everything that is good about my life, my work, and especially my family.

I love you.

CONTENTS

ACKNOWLEDGMENTS

I am so proud of the cover of this book. My daughter Julia took the picture on a hike in the Colorado mountains. It reminds me to be patient to see what happens when the fog lifts and, at the same time, to look harder at what I have and to be thankful. There are so many ways to look at that beautiful picture and be reminded that it's all in the mind.
Thank you, Julia, for always helping me to look at things differently.

OXOX

INTRODUCTION

It was October 8, 2011, and I was in Moab, Utah, for the seventeenth annual 24 Hours of Moab mountain biking race, more specifically "Behind-the-Rocks." I'd never done a twenty-four-hour race of any kind, nor had I ever been to Moab. I was a personal trainer based in Colorado, and I had trained back home for the race for the last twenty weeks. My father, who was very ill with liver cancer, my mother, my partner, and my four kids had come along to cheer me on. My adrenaline was pumping, and I was thrilled! I had played NCAA basketball in college, had spent years as a professional triathlete, and still continued to run races and participate in adventure mud and obstacle events. I felt prepared physically and mentally. I was part of a four-person team, so I had time to rest and strategize with my best friend, Tess. While the first person on our team went out to the fifteen-mile course, I settled into our campsite and ate. Two hours later, it was my turn to head out. I started down a narrow single-track trail, and my family cheered me on as I went for about a quarter mile. The course got sandy, then rocky, then steep and sandy, then rocky, then steep and sandy. At this point, I had to carry my bike over my shoulder and climb what I as a Michigan native would call a very steep sand dune. I was breathing hard, struggling to carry my bike, and wishing I had known to train in the sand. When I got to the top of the hill, the trail evened out somewhat so that I could ride again. After about two miles, I saw yellow "caution" tape and a backboard leaning up against a tree; I felt myself going from excited and bound and determined to scared and unsure of my abilities. As I passed the tree with the backboard, the landscape ahead looked like a minefield of boulders as big as my garage. I would have to cross this on my bike. It looked as though I would have to jump my bike from boulder to boulder. I made a plan to lift up my bike, lower it down below me, then use the bike as a make-shift ladder to support me while lowering my body six feet down to the first boulder. I forged ahead in this way, repeating this process several times. I got banged up, exhausted, and very, very frustrated. Then I looked up to the sky, ready to ask God to help me, and I suddenly saw a guy jumping on his bike from boulder to boulder. That was when I sat down and started to cry. Initially, I thought this race was a good idea and something I could accomplish; now I felt dumb for even entering it. At that moment, I realized I wasn't going to live forever, and I knew dying out in these rocks was not at all how I wanted to go out. I thought about the three hard years I had spent with my adopted Haitian sons and the soon-to-come death of my father. I thought of all the crazy things I had done in my life. I thought a lot because, right then, I could only think. I was too scared to move.

During a therapy session with my youngest Haitian son who was struggling to adapt to the changes in his life, the therapist asked me if I had any limitations, and I said no. You see, that particular day we were discussing a phone call that my partner and I had received in the middle of the night from someone in Haiti, speaking very broken English, telling us that Denzie (9) our son's older brother, had survived the earthquake and needed to be adopted because he was starving and very ill. Of course, this person on the phone wanted $10,000 more, but I heard nothing except the fact that he needed me.

I was sure I was limitless and that was one of the best things about me. I was so limitless that I even risked my life going back to Haiti during a hurricane to help my new kids' family. I believed that if I had an able body and mind, my faith, and good fortune, I could do anything. Now, sitting on that rock in Moab, I wasn't so sure. I had never felt this way before. Did my parents do an amazing job of giving me self-confidence? Was I born feeling as if I had more to give than take? Or was I just crazy? The answers to these questions didn't matter now; I just had to finish this race.

After sitting there for what seemed like forever, I was approached by a guy who asked if I could help him get down off the boulders. That's when I noticed he only had one leg. I immediately snapped out of my own self-pity, and we accomplished the descent together.

Hours later, it was my turn to go again. It was late at night now and pitch-black out, but, amazingly enough, the route was less scary in the dark. I had already done the course once and, if the guy with one leg could do it, then surely I could do it however many more times I needed to for my team. About midnight, I got scared again and let the self-doubt sink in. This is when I hid in the Porta Potty and called my partner. As soon as she answered, I started to cry and told her to come get me, that I didn't want to die out there in the dark, and that I would cheat if I had to. I had come up with a plan to have her drive the big Suburban that we were using to the edge of the course where I would ride my bike down the road and hide myself and my bike in it for a couple hours. Then, I'd cross the finish line and tell everyone that I did the course again. I told her no one would know. I think back on it now and realize how well she knew me because she went along with all of it. She was very supportive and offered her love, but right before we hung up the phone, she said, "Hey, go get some rest and a snack and call me back so we can discuss where to meet." Of course, after her positive words and encouragement, I knew I could never let her, my family, or myself down.

So I got back on my bike, as anyone with a goal would have done, and started up around the corner to the big sand dune and did the course all over again. The yellow caution tape and the backboard were still there, but this time it wasn't scary. My mind-set was different, I was still me and I was still in shape, but this time I used positive self-talk reminded myself that I had already done this once and that I could for sure do it again. At the time, I didn't know what I was doing. Now I do, and guess what—it worked. As I said before, it was less scary in the dark, less competitive, and more of an adventure.

Back at home, I thought I should be happy—happy I finished the race in Moab and happy it was over—but something was different. This event opened up a whole different world to me, a world with limitations. I was now scared of everything in life and felt like the easier route to take with most challenges was to not even try to overcome them. Relationships, work, family, friends, and athletic events no longer seemed important to me. I needed to figure out what these limitations meant.

I went through about two months of watching my father die. It was such a hard thing to do, but at the same time was a great lesson in the true gift of life and the importance of living each day to the absolute fullest. I decided that I needed to really understand what had happened to me in Moab. I went ahead and got my master's degree in sports psychology, thinking the classes would teach me and help me understand my own limitations to overcome them. I would also be able to help my clients recognize their limitations and guide them to reach their goals successfully.

It was the right decision to pursue this course of study. One of the main things I learned about myself is that I simply didn't have the mental skills I had needed to push myself as hard as I did in that event in Moab. If I had worked on visualization, positive self-talk, and self-hypnosis as much as I had worked on my physical training, I would not have experienced that breakdown.

It has been several years now since that race, and I have finished my master's in psychology with a certificate in sports psychology. I also went to school to become a sports hypnotherapist, became a registered psychotherapist in the state of Colorado, and opened my own personal-training studio. I changed my mind-set and my focus after that adventure in Moab. I wanted to add more value to the personal training that I already did by helping others understand how to change their mind-set and break their bad habits. Over the years, I have had many success stories with my clients—weight loss, injury rehab, and increased performance—but the difference between previous successes and those I have now is the long-lasting effects like attitude, motivation, and a life-changing mind-set.

You may think it's too late to make such changes or that it just might be too hard to change yourself. That's where the mind comes in. If you can take steps to change your mind, you are putting yourself on the path to change whatever you want. You can change your mind-set, your health, your strength, and your life. You may feel that you lack the energy or that the environment might not be right for you to be successful, but these are just excuses. Think about a success story that touched you. Maybe it was your neighbor who lost eighty pounds, your friend who overcame her addiction, or your sister who competed in a triathlon. Consider my Haitian sons who have seen the worst our world has to offer. Despite the trauma they've been through, they overcame it all. How did they do it? How are they any different from you? Where did they start? Most likely, just like you, they didn't like their circumstances and wanted to change them.

And how do you change your mind? It begins and ends with exercise. Exercise for your body, exercise for your mind, and exercise for your soul.

1 EXERCISE

Exercise changes how our body works—including our brain. Wendy Suzuki, a neuroscientist, began exercising and discovered that she not only got stronger and fitter but that her mood improved, her memory and attention seemed better, and her productivity increased. Suzuki was so excited about her new research findings that she decided to study how exercise can change the brain's anatomy, physiology, and function. She found that exercise increases one's mood by increasing the levels of serotonin and noradrenalin. It also releases "feel good" chemicals that are associated with pleasure. Dopamine is released in the brain both when someone falls in love and when someone exercises.

Hers and others' research also shows that your attention span increases when you exercise. Exercise increases the growth of red blood cells in the brain. The brain is our number-one consumer of oxygen: the more blood that flows through the brain, the more oxygen it gets. Exercise can literally help your brain grow; there is evidence that the cortex gets thicker with exercise. The thicker the brain cells, the more function there is—the bigger a muscle is, the more function or strength it has.

Exercise and the improvement of overall health that comes from exercise have also been shown to improve synapses in the brain. Synapses are the connections where one neuron communicates with another, so the number and the size of synapses really matter when it comes to effective thinking. Additionally, Suzuki found that exercise increases memory and can even beat stress (Suzuki 2016).

Perhaps the most important thing that exercise can do for our minds is to increase our imaginations. With an increased imagination, we see more possibilities for ourselves. The excuses that keep us from changing our lives begin to fall away. Possibilities that we didn't even know were out there arise when we put one foot in front of the other, and these possibilities show us that we can live a life without limitations.

Exercise has played a role in many success stories. I remember being at a personal-training conference where the speaker came out as well as a woman who was jumping rope. The speaker presented for sixty minutes, and the woman jumped rope the whole time without stopping. After the sixty minutes of jumping rope, the woman explained that three years earlier she had been in a bad car accident, badly injured and lost a loved one, and had given up on life. A friend encouraged her to stop feeling sorry for herself (what I would call "change her mind") and start jumping rope. For this woman, the jump rope changed everything.

For me, exercise has always meant a way to get somewhere else. Let me explain. I have always loved to play. Playing meant I got to be with other people. Whether it was croquet in the backyard with my mom or softball on the local Little League team, playing was fun and competitive, and it motivated me to want to be better. I always thought that getting better at something would open the door to a better life. You see, my parents were always telling my siblings and me that we got one chance at life and that we'd better make it a good one. This was a very powerful message, particularly coming from my superhero dad. My parents knew what they were talking about. They lost their son, Tommy, when he was five. He was riding his bike when a car hit him. This obviously changed everything for my parents, so much so that they never let us forget how precious life is and what our responsibility was in making the most out of it. Even though I never met Tommy, he taught me a lot. He taught me the importance of having fun and taking care of myself. He taught me to love like crazy. I realized that if he wasn't here to do it himself then we all needed to do it for him—extra hugs, extra kisses, and more time spent together, appreciating what we did have. When I played catch with my dad he would often say, "I bet Tommy would love to be playing catch." He'd say the same thing whether we were waterskiing, snowmobiling, or weightlifting, and especially when we played basketball. I took this to heart every time I played anything. To this day, if I run, ski, swim, lift weights, or play pickle ball, Tommy is right there with me. I am playing for him.

I played every sport I could in high school—basketball, tennis, softball. I ran cross country and even played on the boys' soccer team. All this participation in sports opened doors for me. I never would have gone to college if it hadn't been for a basketball scholarship. Today, I have many personal-training certifications and a master's in sports psychology. All these experiences led me to become a personal trainer, in hopes that I could give everyone I meet the same desire, the same mind-set, to do better and be better—to be stronger, fitter, happier, and healthier.

With my twenty-plus years of experience in the health and fitness business, I have seen so many people open doors for themselves by exercising and accomplish things they never thought possible. Over and over, I have seen people change every part of their lives by increasing their activity and making the choice to be in control over their own health and well-being.

One client that I have worked with for years inspires me repeatedly with her drive, determination, and desire to always want to be better, stronger, and fitter. Now in her thirties, she has spent the last ten years as a paraplegic. After a terrible skiing accident that caused a spinal cord injury, she has had to live her life in a totally different way. Instead of choosing to be angry, she has chosen to be a role model and an inspiration. Most likely, she will never walk again, but that doesn't stop her from trying. We come up with stuff all the time in my gym to get her standing or hanging. We laugh a lot when the new exercise doesn't work and celebrate when it does—or at least when it helps her to have less pain. For most of us, paralysis of any sort is something we will never have to worry about, but for her it's a way of life, a much harder life with lots of setbacks and challenges. But with the right mind-set, we can all overcome our challenges. We can all keep moving forward toward feeling better, being more active, and being happier.

Another great example of putting one foot in front of the other comes from another client of mine, a male in his fifties who was extremely overweight. After a divorce, he lost his job and faced a hip replacement. The doctor told him he needed to lose weight or the hip replacement wouldn't work, so he decided to start working with me. At first, there wasn't much we could do that didn't hurt his hip. When I tried to do exercises with him sitting down, there was nowhere for him to sit because he was so large. He was embarrassed to be seen in public and very angry with everyone and everything. I would say he had hit bottom. Gradually, I did find things that we could do, which led to his feeling better, which then led to more things we could do. First, I noticed that he started to smile; he was happy with himself. And then he started to lose weight. When the weight started to drop, so did the pain in his hip. He even got off most of his medication, which saved him a lot of money. That was years ago, and now he is slim, healthy, and has not only a new hip but also an active lifestyle and a new life. It all began with that smile—a sign that he was changing his mind.

It doesn't have to be jump rope, or working out in a gym, it can be anything that gets you moving—walking, running, swimming, biking, or weight lifting. Any regular physical activity can change your mind and put you on the path to the life you want.

What if you don't like to exercise or you don't have access to a gym or moving your body hurts? Then find something you do like and try to modify it into being a good thing for you. For example, many of us like to watch TV, so use the commercial breaks to move. Stand up and sit down for the length of the commercial or simply do arm circles or tap your feet.

It can be big body movements or little movements, but move (and not to the refrigerator!). There are no limitations if you don't place them on yourself. Just start moving and smiling and being thankful for the body you have. Then make the changes necessary for you to be better and feel better.

So, now that we know that we need to change our minds and that exercise is the first step to do this, what is our next step? Everyone needs to start with a goal. A short-term goal, a midrange goal, a slightly harder goal, and a long-term goal are a great place to start. Once you have decided on each of these goals and a timeline, then consider making a very challenging goal. When setting goals, you need to have some that you know without a doubt you can accomplish (like drinking eighty ounces of water a day or stretching every night before you go to bed), but you also need a goal that is so challenging that that goal is the fuel for your fire to accomplish all the others. For example, losing fifty pounds or winning the club championship next year would be big goals that take time and planning. Take a moment to think about a very challenging goal and visualize yourself accomplishing it. How does that feel? What does it mean for your future and your life as a whole? It's important to write these goals down and maybe even discuss them with someone you trust. The more time and thought you put into making these goals, the more likely you will be to stick with them.

"A dream written down with a date becomes a GOAL. A goal broken down into steps becomes a PLAN. A plan backed by ACTION makes your dreams come true. (Money Saving Enthusiast 2014).

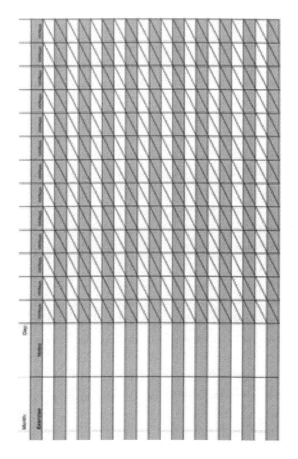

Sample Workout Card: a great example of holding yourself accountable.

2 GOALS

Goal setting is very helpful when getting started on anything new. If you have a goal in mind, then you can start figuring out the steps you need to take to accomplish that goal. Goal setting is a positive psychology skill, a way of focusing your mind that helps improve self-confidence and increases outcomes and performance. A specific goal is needed as a target so that you can focus on reaching that target in a specific amount of time. Goals improve outcomes by keeping your attention and focus on the goal-relevant activities. You may find that it's easier to have a clear objective if you work with a sports psychologist or personal trainer, or you may be able to come to it on your own. Once again, with a clear objective and clearly outlined goals, you will know what steps to take and when to take them. You will have a well-defined path ahead. So let's get started.

1. *Set goals that are measurable.*

What exactly do you want to achieve? When do you want to achieve this goal, and how are you going to do it? You need to break down the goal into measurable elements. Being happier is not a measurable goal because happiness on a day-by-day or hour-by-hour basis is very hard to measure, but losing weight and exercising for forty-five minutes a day is something you can measure. Adding vegetables to your diet and doing more stretching are also measurable goals. (This doesn't mean that you can't ultimately achieve happiness, but you will do so by first achieving smaller, measurable goals.)

Setting measurable goals is very important in refining what exactly it is that you want to accomplish. Defining the objective and really breaking it down makes it clearer and easier to reach.

2. *Set goals in behavioral terms.*

To think in terms of behavioral goals, ask yourself what it would take to achieve this goal. What do you have to do to make it happen? How would your behavior have to change? Those specific actions are your behavioral terms. With the behavioral terms, you are trying to isolate your actions from outside influences. You've set the goal to train for a 5K in six weeks, and you need to commit to exercising for forty-five minutes after work, before you have dinner. Maybe one night your friends want you to go out and celebrate with them after work, but doing so might lead you to making a decision that doesn't fit into the goals and the timeline that you have set for yourself. Now you need to have a plan for if you go or you need to decide that it doesn't work for you to go out at all right now. Another scenario would be that you've set the goal to start going to bed thirty minutes earlier so you can get up thirty minutes earlier to start walking around the block every morning. After a few days of this, you are feeling really good about your goal and your accomplishment, but today it's raining. You ask yourself if you should walk in the rain or do thirty minutes of activity (like squatting and lunging) around the house? Of course, you get to choose, but you understand that doing something is better than hitting the snooze and rolling over. Snoozing would not get you closer to your goal.

3. *Set goals that are hard but realistic.*

"The victory of success is half won when one gains the habit of setting goals and achieving them. Even the most tedious chore will become endurable as you parade through each day convinced that every task, no matter how menial or boring, brings you closer to fulfilling your dreams."
—Og Mandino

I wish someone would have taught me to set goals. Over the years I have made so many mistakes because I didn't have goals. For example, once, I decided to do a very long hike at twelve thousand feet altitude without the proper training and equipment and got myself in a very unsafe situation. Another time, I set some very unrealistic goals for my diet.

Not only were they very difficult to accomplish, but I ended up malnourished. It has taken me a long time to learn how to effectively set realistic goals.

There are a couple things you can do to be successful at keeping your goals on track, making them hard but attainable. Two psychologists, Locke and Latham, did a study about goal setting and found that "specific, difficult goals consistently lead to higher performance than urging people to be their best" (Locke and Latham 1990). The highest or most difficult goals produce the highest levels of effort and performance. So, if you want to lose weight, set a goal for how much weight, a challenging timeline and stick to a specific diet and exercise program. Outline exactly what has to happen for you to accomplish this specific goal. Because you have set specific goals, they direct your attention toward activities that matter and away from distractions. Locke and Latham also state that harder goals energize us. Hard goals lead to greater effort than easier goals. Harder goals also increase and prolong our effort; adding in a deadline makes you work harder and faster to meet that deadline.

4. *Set short, midrange and long-term goals.*

Short-term goals are important because we need to have things to measure and hold ourselves accountable for along the way. With the accomplishment of the short-term goals, we learn to surpass our own self-imposed limitations while building confidence and determination to accomplish the harder longer-term goals.

Midrange goals build from your short-term goals and the accumulation of both of these leads to accomplishing the long-term goal. For example, in order to lose weight, you need trackable weekly goals on how to exercise and what to eat. A specific short-term goal for this would be to stay on track for a week, eating right and exercising. Then, for your midrange goal, you might say you want to lose six pounds in eight weeks. You can then make sure your strategies for exercise and eating have resulted in the midrange weight loss goal. With the short-term and midrange goals in mind, you are better able to stay on track for a six-month weight loss goal.

5. *Set process, performance, and outcome goals.*

These are three distinct types of goals, and separating these goals helps to organize your thought process so you can focus on what you want to accomplish.

Process goals are completely under your control. These are the small steps you take to get to the performance goals and the outcome goals. For example, drinking eighty ounces of water per day, or exercising three times per week for forty minutes each session, or eating less can get you closer to your performance goal.

Performance goals are what you are trying to accomplish in the long run, like losing weight, getting faster, or increasing your strength. Performance goals help you to answer the question of what you expect the outcome to be. It shows you the areas that you should focus your attention to accomplish the goal.

The outcome goal is the big-picture goal that is not always under your control. An example would be that you have done everything on your weight loss plan and achieved both your process goals and performance goals, but your sister still lost more weight than you did in the same amount of time, which was your outcome goal. You could not control your sister and her results. Another example is if you are on track for weight loss at the three-month mark, but then you get pneumonia and are down and out for six weeks and lose momentum. This outcome goal is not based on someone else but is an outside influence.

6. *Tell someone about your goals to help you to stay accountable.*

When you tell a friend or family member about your new goal, they will most likely support you and encourage you when you feel like giving up. When sharing your goal, you have to be very clear about how you are going to accomplish this goal and be accountable to share when and if the goal changes. Telling someone else your new goal can also help you to stay motivated, an added incentive. Sharing your goal with like-minded people can also provide a connection and help grow your social circle. Hanging out with individuals who have a similar goal can help you accomplish yours. When you share your goal and tell someone that you are going to do something, you will be more likely to do it, plain and simple. This is why it good to have a workout partner or get involved in a running group. There are always people who want someone to join them for hiking, playing Frisbee golf, or going for a bike ride.

I really like what Brad Hudson says in his book *Run Faster from the 5K to Marathon*: "Dispel fear of failure, discover your full potential, achieve your personal best by setting big yet attainable goals." Everyone must set goals that are attainable, but what about the times when we fail to reach our goals? That's when we need to "dispel the fear of failure" and turn our mistakes into progress and learning. When you fail to achieve your goal, in whole or in part, turn your unsuccessful attempts into stepping-stones that lead to your final achievement or little victories. When you have poured everything you have into achieving your goal and tried as hard as you can but didn't achieve the end result, you must still be able to see the results and progress you made along the way. For most of us, though, we accomplish our goals because we set goals too low and sabotage ourselves, forgetting we are capable of more than we realize.

3 A POSITIVE MIND-SET

A positive mind-set is essential for improved performance, whether you are aiming for weight loss, increased productivity, or better athletic performance. It is also essential for turning the challenges of your life into opportunities. We all have challenges—some of us more than others. Positive self-talk, visualization, goal setting, mental imagery, and hypnosis are several key components for developing a positive mind-set. They are effective tools to help you redirect your thought processes from negative to positive and to visualize the perfect outcome for yourself. If you can visualize it, if you can direct your positive thinking toward accomplishing it, it will come. This quote inspires me every time I see it: "Think you will fail or think you will succeed; one thing is for sure—one of them will be true." If you think you will succeed, you will make your choices in life that lead you on the path to success. Success will be your truth.

Self-talk is the language inside your head that affects self-worth and performance. Negative self-talk is very harmful to our performance and will lead us away from our goals. If you just stop for a second and listen to what you are saying to yourself, most of the time you will find it to be more negative than positive. The negative thoughts are different for everyone, but many of us can relate to that familiar voice that tells us that we are not good enough, not cute enough, not athletic or popular enough. As we get older, those negative thoughts can turn into not caring and not doing. When we consistently tell ourselves that we need more money or a better house or a nicer car, we prove to ourselves that we really aren't as good as whomever we are comparing ourselves to. At a minimum, this kind of thinking can be distracting to the task at hand and disrupt the automatic performance of a task or skill. At its worst, negative thinking can be downright destructive and, over time, we may hardly even notice that almost all of our thoughts are getting us exactly what we don't want.

Stop for a minute and think about someone you know from school or work who always seems to point out the negative. He or she doesn't view the glass half full but always half empty. If you took the time to point this out, the person most likely would argue that it wasn't true or that it did not matter. The negative thoughts affect both the person and those around them. One summer when I played soccer, there was a woman on the team who seemed to never have things go her way. For most of us on the team, it was easy to see why. As soon as she would get to practice, all she would talk about was the crazy driver on the way over and the terrible job everyone did at work that made her life so much harder. It went on and on, at practice and at the games—everything was unfair, and the officials were always playing favorites on the other team's behalf. I don't know what ever happened to that self-sabotaging woman, but while I knew her, life was not as she hoped, and the rest of us had to work hard to stay in the right mind-set when we were around her. This proves that the energy we spend on anything worthwhile needs to be positive energy—energy that moves us in a direction of positive change and increased happiness.

If negative self-talk is so harmful, what does it's opposite look like? What is positive self-talk? It begins by listening to that quiet inner voice that keeps whispering about a passion unfilled. Self-talk is any time you engage in an internal dialogue with yourself, like interpreting what you are feeling or giving yourself directions. This dialogue can be inside your head or out loud. It can help everyone regulate anxiety, stay focused, and cope better with difficult situations. If you can direct and redirect the thoughts going through your head, then there is decreased self-doubt and increased performance. Self-talk is an important tool for the learning process of any skill or new idea. Self-talk can influence increased performance in many ways—through the acquisition of a new skill, the development of self-regulation of habits, and building self-confidence. Self-regulation of habits means the ability to stop yourself from doing those often unconscious things that are not good for us, like biting our nails or thinking bad thoughts. Taking the leap from negative to positive self-talk is tricky at first, but it will be much easier if you trust yourself. Every time a negative thought pops into your head, you need to have the skills to stop the thought or redirect it to a better way of thinking. To help you understand how negative thoughts affect you, keep track of your thoughts for a whole day. Carry with you a notecard and a pen, and every time you catch yourself with a negative thought (self-talk), put a check mark on the card. At the end of the day, count how many negative thoughts you had. If you like, you can get more specific by keeping track of what the thought was related to and at what time of day it occurred (for example, are you at work, looking in the mirror, driving in the car?). On day two, tell yourself the minute you get up in the morning that today will be different, more positive, and you will be more caring, and more aware of your thoughts. On day two, it's important to keep track on the note card again to see what is hopefully a much more positive day. Again, you can be more specific about your feelings, energy level, and overall happiness, if you like. This little exercise will help you better understand the importance of redirecting negative, self-doubting thoughts to positive ones.

Awareness

Negative

Positive

Self-talk is based on the use of cues, which help activate appropriate and desired responses like "You got this" or "Go for it." A cue can be anything that is said or done that serves as a signal or reminder of the desired action or behavior that you would like to change or have happen. These cues can be verbalizations that you address to yourself (for example: "Stay focused," "You can do this," or "Yes, I can.") What you are really doing is giving yourself instructions and reinforcements; you perceive what you are feeling.

Another important cue is one that triggers you to stop negative thoughts, also referred to as thought stoppage. This cue makes you aware of negative thoughts as soon as they rise up so that you can stop them immediately before they set you on the wrong path, away from progress. For the thought stoppage to occur, you need to choose a word, like *stop*, *delete*, or *cancel* or use an action like snapping your fingers when you become aware of negative thoughts. When you get up in the morning, be aware of the things you are saying to yourself. If it sounds like anything less than uplifting and positive, say "Cancel," "Delete," and "Start over," or move on to better thoughts about what you are going to accomplish and enjoy in your day.

An example of this process at work would be when you are driving to work, going over in your mind the day ahead, and someone pulls out in front of you. Not only did this scare you, but also now you are mad and yelling. In this situation, you need to regulate yourself and your feelings. A good way to do this is by being thankful that nothing bad happened and start repeating one of the positive affirmations that you have taught yourself. "Happiness does not depend on what you have or who you are; it solely relies on what you think" -Buddha. As you get better at stopping the negative thoughts, you will get better at having a quiet mind and saying more positive things to yourself.

There are different types of self-talk beyond just positive and negative. Instructional self-talk is used to help performance or behavior by triggering wanted movement through correct focus, technique, and strategy implementation (Williams 2010). In other words, you are talking yourself through all the steps of a new task or a behavior that you would like to change. If it's a sports skill, maybe you tell yourself to see the target, breathe, check your posture, aim, and shoot. The results of using the self-talk technique can be (but are not limited to) increased focus, greater self-confidence, and the ability to break down complex activities that require great skill or knowledge and perform them with more success.

Instructing yourself through a task also means you gain a better understanding of what exactly you need to do. That doesn't mean the task will be easy, but it does mean you have a greater knowledge of how to do it. Consider the example of losing weight again. In order to lose weight, you need to change your lifestyle, which includes being aware of the food you eat, when and why you eat it, and the way you eat it, as well as being aware of the activity you do, the rest you take, and the mental attitude that you have about it. So to get started on this task, you would set a goal, plan out each day's meals, and have an exercise plan. The instructional self-talk you will use when things get hard also needs to be planned out. For instance, before you go to bed, use a weight loss guided hypnosis recording to help stay on track, and then when you wake up in the morning, have a planned affirmation to repeat to yourself ten times. This can be anything that makes you feel strong and motivated to make good healthy choices.

Some examples are:

- "I love eating healthy food that helps me to reach my ideal weight,"
- "I love exercising daily, and it helps me reach my ideal weight,"
- "Every day and in every way, I am getting slimmer and fitter."

You don't have to use these specific examples but use whatever works for you. The affirmations offer us a chance to stay positive and to avoid the distractions that happen in our everyday lives. Attitude is a part of all the steps.

"A bad attitude is like a flat tire, if you don't change it, you'll never go anywhere." -Anonymous

After you have a goal and a mental game plan, you need a plan of action for drinking lots of water and exercising first thing in the morning (so there are no excuses later). You decide on what snacks and meals you will be eating. You also practice a self-talk technique that you can do anywhere and anytime, so that you have a plan for mentally staying on track. One cue that I think works well for many clients is "Nothing tastes as good as slim feels." Say that a few times to yourself, and you can almost feel what it's like not to have your muffin top hang over your jeans. If that doesn't work for you, then remember what Dr. Dorothy Harris said: "The only difference between the best performance and the worst performance is the variation in our self-talk and the self-thoughts and attitudes we carry around with us" (Williams 2010). So whatever you decide to say to yourself, remember that those words are entirely up to you and that soon your feelings will match your words. Make the self-talk good, uplifting, and positive. Another cue that works well to encourage you to drink more water is the "solution to pollution is dilution," reminding you that the more water you drink, the healthier and more efficient you become. As you can see, there are many steps to setting a goal and being successful in following through on it. Once you have a successful plan of action that works for you, you can then use that same plan of action for the next goal you set.

The other type of self-talk—motivational self-talk—will help you increase performance or success by bumping up your effort and confidence, driving you to use more energy, and improving your mood. Motivational self-talk is positive phrases that encourage you to keep going, stay on track, and work through challenges, even the most difficult ones. These positive cues or phrases can be used to get you psyched up or help you calm down.

Sometimes, the cues help you to stay the course, put one foot in front of the other, and keep going. Examples of motivational positive self-talk to get your energy primed are: "Let's go," "You can do it," and "Get fired up." Statements like "I'm OK" and "Take a deep breath" are motivational self-talk that can help you relax and let go of building tension and anxiety during unfamiliar situations. To help you concentrate on the task at hand, you may simply say to yourself "Focus," and, by repeating the word over and over, you can slow your breathing and relax. These positive statements can boost self-confidence, enhance self-efficacy, improve mood, and remove nervous feelings. Self-talk occurs any time you engage in an internal dialogue with yourself, like interpreting what you are feeling or giving yourself directions. This dialogue can be inside your head or said out loud. It can help regulate anxiety and arousal, and help you stay focused and cope better with difficult situations. If you can direct and redirect the thoughts going through your head while in competition or while trying to make a behavior change, you will perform a lot better.

Choose statements that are vivid and easily roll off your tongue. Practice the self-talk phrases you choose on a regular basis. Make a list of four or five positive self-statements. Read them to yourself every night before you go to bed and then again every morning before you get up. The more you practice them, the more they will become embedded in your unconscious mind so that positive thoughts will guide your every action all day long, helping you to get closer to your goals and aspirations.

Here are some examples of positive self-talk statements for various situations:

Situation	Statement
Basketball free-throw shooter	"It's just me and the basket."
In an interview	"I am the one for the job."
Ski-jumper	"My timing is always spot on."
Weight loss	"Exercise makes me feel great."
Road biker	"The hills make me stronger."
Jogger	"I am so lucky to have the body to do this."
Those with fitness goals	"I am getting stronger and healthier with every step."
For success	"I have a great vision for my future, and I will no longer allow my fears to interfere with my success."

HYPNOSIS

As you can see, there are many different tools and skills that you can develop to keep yourself on track and make positive changes in your life. Having an open mind is essential to discovering what works best for you. Using positive self-talk and breathing techniques work well for many people, but for some there is more success in changing their mind-set and actions with hypnosis.

Many people think of hypnosis as stage hypnosis, where people from an audience volunteer to come up on stage to be hypnotized to cluck like a chicken or have their feet stuck to the floor so that they can't move. This is not what I am referring to. You may also think about a watch swinging back and forth and Gilligan going into a deep trance and doing funny things on the old show *Gilligan's Island*. Though this watch method is still used today if that's the technique the therapist believes will get the client's focus and attention, it is not the only method.

The theory of hypnosis is based on the writings of Milton H. Erickson, who says that hypnosis is an altered state of consciousness. It is a psychological state that is very similar to visualization, which means to recall or form mental images or pictures, but usually is more effective if the individual is in a deeper state of relaxation. The biggest benefit of hypnosis is that, following the brief period of relaxation, you can now adopt more positive attitudes toward yourself, your performance, training, and competition.

Another definition of hypnosis is a procedure during which a hypnotherapist suggests that a client experience changes in sensations, perceptions, thoughts, or behavior. A suggestion allows you to experience a sort of imaginary state (e.g., "You are feeling calm, confident, in control, and powerful as you imagine yourself hitting the ball off the tee."). Another term often used is hypnotic trance, where there is access to different functions of the brain. What you can expect when you first try hypnosis is an interview process with the therapist. This consists of questions and answers that help the therapist understand better what you are feeling and hoping for in the hypnosis session. Once the interview is over, you and the therapist move to a comfortable place to relax, maybe there is a fountain going or some light music and dim lighting. The therapist can choose to do many different types of hypnotic inductions to get you more relaxed (like keeping your eye on a watch, deep breathing, or having you follow the therapist's hand). All this does is help you to focus on what you are here for in the first place. Have you ever gotten into your car and driven to a certain place and, when you got there, you couldn't remember getting there? That was a form of hypnosis just like daydreaming. The subconscious mind was already programmed to drive to the destination, and there was no need for the conscious mind to get involved. There is nothing to be afraid of when trying hypnosis because you cannot be talked into anything that your mind is not ready to accept. The therapist can make suggestions, and you can accept them or not. It's that easy! It's basically an hour of relaxing while the therapist is making suggestions that make you feel good, empowered, and strong.

Hypnosis can increase the opportunity to understand unconscious motivations of your own actions such as why is it so important to want to lose weight or get rich at any cost. There are so many things that hypnosis can help with. I have seen people with anxiety and self-loathing become free of these feelings and move on with their lives in a very healthy manner. Understanding unconscious motivations can help you determine a course of action and what treatment goals are needed. Hypnosis also allows greater access to the functions of the right side of the brain. The basic characteristics of the right side of the brain (including creativity, imagination, intuition, feelings, visualization, and daydreaming [Scull 2010]) are very important when we talk about sports performance and increased overall health.. Most of us agree that life is too short, so having a skill that helps us feel more playful, positive, and focused is a great skill to have.

There are numerous reports of famous athletes using hypnosis to enhance sports performance. Tiger Woods and Nolan Ryan have both been published talking about their sports hypnosis experience and have even gone as far as explaining that working with a sports psychologist and doing hypnosis helped them to experience less pain. The Denver Broncos also report having team and individual success using a sports psychologist and self-hypnosis skills. Mary Lou Retton used hypnosis to block the pain in her foot and ankle and won the gold medal for USA gymnastics in 1984. There is validated evidence-based science demonstrated on brain imaging to prove what Mary Lou Retton was able to do during the Olympics (Wehbe and Safar 2015). Pro golfer Jack Nicklaus has said that hypnotherapy and visualization techniques are the sole reason for his improved concentration. For an athlete who makes money performing his or her sport, having any kind of an edge might be the thing that keeps bringing the money home. Hypnosis can change your way of thinking and add confidence and motivation to any new goal. Hypnosis can help you see and feel things differently. Hypnosis can also stop bad behaviors and break long-lasting habits. This can be an additional resource for anyone trying to make a lifestyle change and improve performance in any area of life that he or she chooses to concentrate on.

SELF-HYPNOSIS

Self-hypnosis is when you yourself use autosuggestion to help your mind-set become more open and yielding to new ideas and ways of thinking. If you don't know where to start, start at the beginning. Tell yourself over and over that you love yourself and that you will make the changes necessary to better your current situation. Most of us know exactly what would make our lives better, healthier, and more enjoyable but lack the power to really make the change. There is no doubt that change is hard and takes you out of your comfort zone, but the saying that "You're not living until you get outside your comfort zone" is very true. Think about a time when you have really reached past what was comfortable; most likely you discovered something great. Self-hypnosis uses positive self-talk messages to get into a trance-like state more effectively, but it is very different from what we are trying to accomplish when we use a cue word, which helps us get back to a better way of thinking. Self-hypnosis is hypnosis that is a heightened state of suggestibility that we have brought upon ourselves. For some, this is easier said than done, and that is why they continue to see a hypnotherapist. For others, they can use a phrase, cue word, or touch their first finger to their thumb (if that is their trigger), or a simple affirmation to get themselves more relaxed and in a deeper state of consciousness. Most of us don't get as deep as we would if we had a therapist leading the hypnosis session. But by having the skills to use self-hypnosis, we can calm ourselves, self-regulate during a competition, or use to avoid temptations.

In summary, self-hypnosis is using positive self-talk to induce a deeper feeling of relaxation or peace so that you're in a state that you can better utilize the imagery skills you already have. There are many resources for hypnosis and self-hypnosis. You can go see a hypnotherapist, watch or listen to videos, and refer to many different types of hypnosis books. Hypnosis can help you feel less anxious and scared, help with weight loss, and increase your focus. The best part of hypnosis is that it can do anything that you want it to. You just have to open yourself to it.

Steps to entering into self-hypnosis:
1. Close your eyes and hum lightly to rid your mind of any feelings of fear, stress, or anxiety.
2. Recognize any tension in your body.
3. Take slow, deep breaths.
4. Appreciate the fact that you are now extremely relaxed.
5. Feel heavy sensations in your arms and legs as you become more relaxed.
6. Repeat these steps as many times as you wish.

POSITIVE AFFIRMATIONS

There are more times in my life than I would like to admit when I have felt fearful, lost, and scared of what the future will bring, while being disappointed in my choices in the past. This is a heavy burden, but there are ways to let yourself feel these feelings and then move on. Positive affirmations help you move on from any negative thoughts or feelings. As you begin to rely on them even more, they can become a preventive measure. There is a saying I keep on my desk to look at every day: "At work, my mind is focused, and I have clarity and energy in all that I do."

Positive affirmations are sayings or statements that reflect thoughts and attitudes about yourself. The statements need to be believable and vivid. Using positive affirmations helps to stop negative thoughts from taking over and decreasing your performance. The power of suggestion is much like a drug in that its potency improves if you take it on a consistent basis. One source of affirmations is to download an app for your mobile device that gives you a new affirmation every day. You may not relate to all of them, but you will find one or two that are appropriate for what you are going through or working on. When you do practice affirmations, believe in them, and they can change your way of thinking. You can always use your own affirmations—they don't have to come from someone else. No one knows yourself better than you do, and you can never dream too big.

"Quitters never win and winners never quit" works for most of us; life is a marathon and not a sprint. Much changes along the way, but we all can focus on being more peaceful and happy. The affirmations can be very simple like "I know I can" or more in-depth like "Every day and in every way I get better and better at…." You just need to be consistent with using them. The skill of using positive affirmations is a lot like positive self-talk, but here you find a favorite quote, memorize it, and then try to incorporate it into your life on a daily basis. A positive affirmation effectively tells our subconscious mind the kind of life we wish to have. This differs from positive self-talk because self-talk helps change a thought we are having now while the repeated affirmations change our overall pattern of thinking.

Examples:
- "The future depends on what you do today."—Gandhi
- "Ability is what you are capable of doing. Motivation determines what you do. Attitude determines how well you do it."—Lou Holtz
- "Anything you really want, you can attain, if you really go after it."—Wayne Dyer

- "Do just once what others say you can't do, and you will never pay attention to their limitations again."—James R. Cook
- "Efforts and courage are not enough without purpose and direction."—John F. Kennedy
- "He who is outside his door has the hardest part of his journey behind him."—Dutch Proverb
- "In the middle of a difficulty lies opportunity."—Albert Einstein

VISUALIZATION

Visualization or mental imagery refers to the process of using your imagination to see yourself performing a movement (e.g. running) or a certain skill (e.g. catching a high ball in rugby or heading the ball in soccer). To do this, you can have your eyes open or closed, and then recreate a thought or image in an attempt to create a better way of thinking, feeling, or doing. This can also be visual or nonvisual, such as images sounds, smells, tastes, touch (incorporating texture, temperature, and pressure). It can also be seeing yourself in different types of clothes and feeling energetic and happy. There are many benefits of using mental imagery skills; they include increased self-confidence, concentration, and skill improvement.

My favorite thing to visualize is a beach scene. Whenever I need to relax, it's always my go-to. It goes something like this: imagine you are walking on the beach, you can hear the waves, smell the ocean spray, and feel the wind lightly moving the shirt you are wearing. As you walk along the empty beach, you notice the bright blue-green color of the ocean and see the waves washing up onto the sand then recede back over and over. Feeling your feet in the nice warm sand, you now walk closer to the water, and let the cool water wash over your feet, feeling instant relief from the hot sun. Next, you go for a swim or lie in the sun, whatever continues the feeling of relaxation.

Visualization is a great way to elicit relaxation, and it can be very helpful in a stressful situation. With your imagination, you can be anywhere or feel anything. For some reason, it's always easier to visualize something bad and be able to feel it right away, but the opposite can be true, too. If you visualize yourself as energetic and happy, you will start to feel energetic and happy—and better yet, you won't allow yourself to be put into a situation that doesn't help you feel energetic and happy. Athletes use visualization skills to help perform their skills better and more consistently. Anyone can use this skill to improve their performance in anything like public speaking, asking their boss for a raise, or having a difficult conversation with a loved one. See yourself having a conversation with your partner that is calm and productive, maybe there is not a final resolution but you both were heard and you both walk away feeling loved and appreciated.

It is so important for individuals and athletes to understand how much they can increase sports or skill performance without having to break down the body any further or increase the chance for injury. Mental imagery skills can be used to recreate the movement, skill, or a not-yet achieved performance, and one can do this at any time and any place. By using information stored in the long-term memory, an individual can rehearse a specific skill and even try a new skill. It makes sense that you need to see where you are going before you can get there, so practicing the skill of visualization will improve performance and increase confidence. The more vivid the imagination, the better you are at using the visualization skill. Thus, for some this is a very easy skill to learn, and, for others, it can be very difficult.

To start using the skill of visualization, generate a mental image from a memory or a fantasy. Then try to intentionally maintain the image. Spend some time keeping the image alive. Once you have the image, you need to examine the details. For example, what are the specifics of the image—its colors, sound, smells, feelings, textures, and so forth. When you have done all three of these things, you need to fix or transform any negative parts of the image into positive ones. The negative parts are those that bring doubt, pain, or another negative emotion. Bringing about this change can be a very worthwhile process that becomes self-altering, giving you a new positive way of thinking and feeling.

4 GIVING BACK, FAITH, ACCOUNTABILITY

As you have read here, there are many ways we can change our minds about something and ultimately end up changing our lives. If you have ever watched *American Ninja Warrior*, you've heard many stories of weight loss, disease, the loss of a loved one, and other life events that have inspired people to change their lives and focus and work really hard to accomplish their physical goals. You may not aspire to become the next ninja warrior, but you are definitely able to give back. You can share your time and talents with others and hold fast to your faith. And, through doing these things, you improve more as you hold yourself accountable.

Who can forget the last words of Steve Jobs, one of the most successful and richest men in the world? He implored us not to seek wealth but to "treasure your family love, love for your spouse, love for your friends…treat everyone well and stay friendly with your neighbors." He explained that "God has made us one way. We can feel the love in the heart of each of us, and not illusions built by fame or money, like I made in my life—I cannot take them with me.I can only take with me the memories that were strengthened by love. This is the true wealth that will follow you, will accompany you; he will give strength and light to go ahead" (Isaacson, 2011).

Many of us think that the grass is greener on the other side, but think about Steve Jobs for a moment. He had more money and fame than most, yet he seems to be telling us that the secret to true success, to living our fullest life is in loving, in giving back. When you take the time to help someone other than yourself, you will feel greatly rewarded. Many of us can be in a crowded room and still feel empty, but when you give of your talents there is a fulfillment that happens. This feeling can change your mind-set, your overall self-worth, and, yes, your life. I'm not sure that when I adopted my sons from Haiti I was exactly thinking that I was giving back, but in the seven years that I have had them, I have heard people say that a lot. I stepped out of my comfort zone and took a huge leap into the unknown. I am sure that the expense, stress, and pain were worth it for my family, my adopted sons, and me. I went to Haiti and came back a changed person, changed in the way I now look at poverty and need, in the way I see broken and lost souls, and in the way I see and feel love. You see, because of the giving that I did and the sacrifices I and my family made, we are now loved by my sons in a way I would have never known if I hadn't taken the chance to give more of myself and my love. My sons were more broken and abused than I have ever heard of anyone being, and they choose to stand up humbly and lovingly to whatever comes their way. They end up teaching the rest of us what it really means to give back and have faith and hang in there. I am not saying that this is what everyone should do, but I do know firsthand of the rewards of giving back.

Giving back can look different for all of us; it can be big, small, expensive, or very time consuming. If you are a people person, then spending time with people in need is a great way to give back. If that does not interest you, maybe you could find an outdoor project that requires your talents or some animals that could use your time and attention. When you give back, it's not just your emotional health that improves, but your overall health does as well. As Bernard Meltzer said, "There is no better exercise for your heart than reaching down and helping to lift someone up."

When you're generous to others, you're more generous to yourself, and that feels good. According to researchers at the University of California-Los Angeles, transformation happens at the cellular level and boosts everything from your psychological outlook to your heart and immune system. Doing service work can also connect you with other like-minded individuals and get you off the sofa. People who volunteer are resourceful, creative, and have better staying power on the job, meaning that if you volunteer more, you will increase your job performance.

"Now faith is confidence in what we hope for and assurance about what we do see."—Hebrews 11:1

Faith. Whatever yours is, use it.

"I have learned that Faith means trusting in advance what will only make sense in reverse."—Philip Yancey

For many people, their faith is the foundation of all their decisions. So pray, meditate, and always ask for guidance. Believing in something bigger than yourself is a great way to put yourself in front of a power that helps us want to be better and more loving. The power of prayer helps us to stay positive and reach the goals we have set for ourselves. Prayer isn't just about asking for something; it's about being thankful for the things we already have. Gratitude is the foundation for us to return the kindness we have received. We are very lucky to have whatever we have because our lives could always be worse. If your faith is bigger than your fears, then you can always keep moving ahead. The journey might not always be easy, but having faith makes it possible.

Your belief system does not have to match mine to hear what I am saying, because the faith I am speaking of here is seeing light with your heart when all your eyes can see is darkness and fear.

Finally, an essential element to changing your mind and changing your life is being accountable. Be accountable to yourself or create a support system that will help you stay on task. It's much easier to go back the way we came than to plow a new path; having a plan or a person or group to stay accountable to will be very important to maintain momentum. Knowing what services are available in your area that align with your goals can also be helpful.

Running and biking groups are easy to find—just try a sporting goods store or athletic shoe store since they often have a group. You can join a gym or recreation center. By finding a group or gym, you become connected to others, and this also helps hold you accountable. It might be the front desk person asking about your workout or a person in the running group that counts on you to be there—either one will help you accomplish your goals. Check with your local community center for diet groups. It is likely that whatever your interest is, you can find someone else with a common goal who also needs someone to help hold him or her accountable.

You may also keep a chart to hold yourself accountable, to check in with yourself each day and make sure you are checking off the tasks that you need to complete to stay on course. Keep in mind that the days are sometimes long but the years are short. This will help you put aside your excuses and keep moving.

A FEW MORE THOUGHTS

I ask myself every day what it is that I can do or say today to get my clients to fully commit. What if there were an easier way for me to get them to buy into the fact that taking better care of themselves would result in a better and different life? What stands in their way—fear, laziness, lack of understanding? There always needs to be more effort and fewer excuses. A desire for something better is the first step, but there is still much work to be done to follow through. I see so many people who have the desire to change but lack the ability to see it through. Focus and concentration are essential in accomplishing a goal of any kind. These are skills that need to be learned and practiced.

I recently spent five one-hour sessions with a husband and wife in their late seventies. They had focus because, you see, they didn't have a choice anymore. The husband was having trouble with his pacemaker and spent most of his time in arterial fibrillation, and the wife had gotten overweight, had balance issues, and was sedentary. In those five sessions, they changed their lives by starting to move more, eating better, and lifting weights. Both of them improved their balance enough to get rid of their canes. Still, there must be a way to teach focus and concentration even when it's not a matter of life and death.

If you have a goal and the motivation to accomplish that goal, then you will also need the skills to shut out all the distractions and temptations so you can succeed. This is where your positive self-talk, support group, and faith will lend a hand. Ask for help from the higher power you believe in so you see things differently and think of things differently. This is a very powerful thing to ask, so be open to what you hear. Come up with a positive saying or mantra to be repeated every time things get hard or you feel like giving up. For example, you could say, "Let it go" or "Just breathe." Something I heard in yoga one day has always stuck with me: "I play, I create, I succeed." Find something positive, uplifting, and directional like that that you can repeat over and over to yourself. Rely on your support system to keep you accountable. You should feel supported and cared for even when you don't feel like you have what it takes to do what is necessary for yourself. Of course, you also need to know it's important to recognize when it's time to ask for help.

Changing your mind about something and then changing your life is no small feat, so having a strong foundation and a set of life skills is the best start. And once again, I think the foundation must include an exercise plan. I believe exercise and physical health are mandatory to really changing your life. If you already exercise and eat healthy, there is always an area in which you could improve. Keeping your body healthy is not a game that has an absolute end goal like bowling where you can score a perfect three hundred. There are always ways to improve our health, like getting to bed earlier, eating fewer processed foods, doing more cardiovascular exercise, or even reducing the stress in our lives whenever we can. Shutting out the negativity and thinking more positively is also a necessary foundation for change and a key to having a peaceful and balanced life.

This may be a new way of thinking for you but think of it like brushing your teeth. It may sound silly, but think about it—how many times a day do you brush your teeth? Most people brush in the morning, sometimes after lunch, and then again before they go to bed. If you have a date or special occasion, you may even brush more than that. You do this because you want to have fresh breath, and you don't want your teeth to rot or your mouth to develop gum disease. This habit is very similar to what I am talking about. We need to take care of our mental health and physical health as much as our dental health. You wouldn't go a day without brushing your teeth, so don't go a day without exercising or relaxing and doing positive mental imagery or positive self-talk.

Unfortunately, everyone reading this has had something bad, sad, or even tragic happen to them or someone they know. Have you ever wondered why some people crumble and others excel when faced with hard times? There are many different reasons for why people handle trauma differently, but it is my conviction that being in good physical and mental health is the best way to face day-to-day challenges and tragedy and not only survive but thrive.

Let me take you back one more time to my adopted Haitian sons. While in a Haitian orphanage, both of them endured so much neglect and abuse and saw things most of us don't see in a lifetime. One of my sons acts as though he will never recover from it, and my other son works harder at everything because of the past pain and suffering. I won't pretend to know the answer to this, but I will forever help both of my sons get stronger and help them to gain the skills to be happy, healthy, and safe. A healthy mind, body, and spirit are the foundation to survive whatever life throws at you. To thrive in your lifetime, you need to practice many of the things that I have mentioned. Eat healthy, nutrient rich foods, exercise, and keep your muscles and bones strong. Positive self-talk, gratitude, and a vision will keep you on track, even when you think you can't take anymore. But don't go it alone! Hopefully, by now you can see that a support

system is very helpful and can keep you focused.
With a willingness to change and by working on
making yourself healthier and stronger, both
physically and mentally, you too can experience the
change you desire.

"Peace is the result of retraining your mind to process
life as it is, rather than as you think it should be."—
Wayne W. Dyer

Works Cited

Hudson, Brad. Run Faster from the 5K to the
Marathon: How to be Your Own Best Coach.

Isaacson, W. (2011). *Steve Jobs.* New York: Simon &
Schuster.

Locke, E. A. and Latham, G. P., eds. *A Theory of
Goal Setting & Task Performance*. Vol. 1.
Englewood Cliffs, NJ: Prentice-Hall, 1990.

Money Saving Enthusiast. "Money Saving Tips."
http://moneysavingenthusiast.com

Suzuki, Wendy A. "10 Ways a Workout Changes
Your Brain." Mind Body Green. Last modified
May 13, 2015.
http://www.mindbodygreen.com/0-18491/10-
ways-a-good-workout-changes-your-brain.html.

Williams, J. M., ed. *Applied Sport Psychology,* 6th ed. New York: Human Kinetics, 2010.

ABOUT THE AUTHOR

Jacqueline Kelly has been a certified personal trainer for over twenty years and recently finished her master's in sports psychology. She owns her own business, Kelly Performance and Wellness. She and her partner have four children and two dogs and live in Colorado. They enjoy paddle boarding, skiing, golfing, and pickle ball. You can visit her website at kellyperformancewellness.com where you can also stay tuned for future writings.

Made in the USA
Columbia, SC
16 January 2020